My Bipolar Manager

SIDNEY S. PRASAD

DEDICATION

I dedicate this book to my very special friend, Gursharn.
Words can't express what an amazing soul you are. Thank
you for being there for me and helping me stay sane while
working for My Bipolar Manager.

CONTENTS

Acknowledgments   i

1   Bipolar   1

2   History Of Bipolar Managers   12

3   What Planet Are They From?   23

4   You're As Good As Your Last Sale   28

5   Can A Nut Sell Ice To An Eskimo?   38

6   Power Trip   47

7   The Art Of Eavesdropping   56

8   Why Are They So Miserable?   68

9   Who Hired These Guys?   80

10   Get Out And Get Even!   89

ACKNOWLEDGMENTS

My heart goes out to all those unfortunate people who are jaded from working for their bipolar managers. I share your pain and understand that it's bad enough every time we turn on our television, we are bombarded with infomercials and stories of people who quit their jobs and now earn millions flipping real estate and selling Forex. I agree with you that life is tough, no matter how we phrase it. It's even infinitely harder getting our asses out of bed Monday morning. Being stuck going to work to a dead-end job, earning a fraction of what we truly deserve. Then, to complete our puzzle of misery, our employers force us to report to a bipolar manager who makes our lives a living hell.

Early in life, we get sold on a false philosophy that our colleagues are our second family. I guess this translates "earning a crappy wage" as a reward for being part of a dysfunctional family. When you really break it down, we spend a third of our lives working for a bipolar manager. Then we spend another third of our lives drowning our sorrows, trying to forget about our bipolar manager and our miserable work environment. The final third of our lives is spent sleeping — sort of like an eight-hour temporary vacation from our thoughts about our bipolar manager. You are not alone, as I have spent the last two decades working for mentally unfit bipolar managers. Let me attempt to remove some of your pain and entertain you with tales that revolve around My Bipolar Manager.

1 BIPOLAR

You're probably wondering how someone inherits the title "bipolar manager." Let's start off by defining the term from a clinical standpoint. Bipolar is a term loosely thrown around by society to describe a person's behavior. But if one were to cross-reference a bipolar disorder in a medical dictionary, they would discover that it is an illness that typically has cycles of depression. At times, one's mood can gradually or rapidly change from low to high. Mood swings can be triggered from the tiniest issues without a valid reason. This sort of disorder can affect thinking, judgment, and behavior. (Please note that there is no disrespect to anyone who is suffering a mental illness or is mentally unstable.)

A manager can be conceptualized as the person responsible for controlling and administering a specific area or an entire company. One component of managerial duties is usually directing and monitoring the work of a group of people. Communication is a large part of the managerial role, no matter if it's with superiors, subordinates, other departments or clients. In layman's terms, a manager is essentially the person who cracks the whip every now and then, ensuring that you are tossing the fries and flipping the burgers or whatever your prescribed duties are.

"How can anyone get angry listening to Bobby McFerrin?"

—Sidney S. Prasad

However, it seems like almost every workplace has a bipolar manager on their payroll. Have you ever worked for someone who, for no apparent reason, will rip a strip off you and then, five minutes later, invite you for a drink and act like nothing happened? Two of the most distinctive characteristics of a bipolar manager are short-term memory and sheer ignorance. Nothing is more entertaining than watching your bipolar manager fail the memory test.

Consider the following scenario that happened at my last sales gig, selling janitorial supplies. My Bipolar Manager, Iman S. Hole, was famous for always being forgetful. One day, he assigned me a specific duty, and then two hours later, he pulled me into the boardroom. He interrogated me on why I went over his bald head and took it upon myself to complete a specific task. I then ran to my desk and printed a copy of the email that clearly specified the assignment. He then laughed and said that he forgot.

I thought to myself that I would like to respond like this: "Forgot, my ass; you just wanted to take out your sexual frustrations out on me, you friggen Nazi."

I had several code names for my boss that my colleagues and I would use to make fun of him behind his dumb ass, such as "Charlie Brown" and "Freak Show." But the classic name was "Nazi," and apparently he was half German, which added a little spice to the situation. When I would get really pissed off at him, I would create a screen saver picture of Hitler, then leave my computer monitor on while I went on a break. I'm quite confident he got the message that he portrayed the "seven bad habits of ineffective mangers" from my books.

"Elevators go up and down, just like your mood swings!"

—Sidney S. Prasad

Suppose Iraq dropped a bomb in Washington, and said, "Oops! It was an accident." Could they get away with an apology? A signature character trait of a bipolar manager is they shoot their missiles at the wrong targets and justify it with a generic "sorry" or "oops."

My Bipolar Manager, Iman S. Hole, was notorious for missing the fine details before launching his missiles. One day, Iman S. Hole called me to his desk and gave me shit for twenty minutes for dropping my pants on the price of a product. After he finished his childish rant, I proceeded with the following statement:

"I can totally appreciate your thoughts on this transaction. However, if I can direct your attention to the bottom right of the invoice, you will clearly notice the name Liz Bien, who was the salesperson that drafted this invoice and executed the transaction."

Then, like the flick of a light switch, Iman S. Hole's bipolar mood swung into normal "sane mode" and he laughed it off.

What grinds my gears with the above scenario is I got stuck absorbing My Bipolar Manager's negative energy for twenty minutes while the rightful person who should have gotten shit got away scot-free with a friendly "try to pay attention to the price in the future."

Does it feel like Halloween every day at your workplace? I ask this question because bipolar managers are full-time energy vampires. They pour out so much negative energy onto their employees and the only way they can survive is to leech the positive energy of the remaining employees who they haven't dumped on yet. In a bipolar manager's mind, they strongly feel that he or she is the poster child for positive energy.

"Positive thinking doesn't work when you're about to shit your pants."

—Sidney S. Prasad

My colleagues and I had a good laugh one day when Iman S. Hole demonstrated that his so-called positive energy resembled a glass of water. He poured a half-glass of orange juice into the water, which was supposed to represent his employee's negative attitude. I wanted to tell the guy to go blow his dad, but he was a bastard child. I guess his dad must have run out of the hospital when the doctor refused to stick him back in his mom's *punanee* when he was born. Too bad life wasn't like the Flintstones, where a friendly stork would deliver the babies. If you don't like what you received, just send it back with the Roadrunner. Oh, wait — those are two different cartoons.

It's really funny how a lot of bipolar managers will preach the expression of "leaving your problems at the door" when arriving to work. But they never seem to practice what they preach. For instance, a bipolar manager will get angry for the sake of getting angry. (You're probably thinking this doesn't make any sense.) The message that I am trying to convey is that most bipolar managers live miserable, lonely lives and enjoy taking it out on others. I don't know if it's because their teacher never called on them when they had their little grubby hand up in junior high, or they are so miserable because the other little shits on the playground didn't accept them growing up. Most bipolar managers are famous for harboring some sort of anger and hostility, and without notice will shift their impulses to an innocent bystander.

"My Bipolar Manager is the only guy in the world that gets angry when eating a Happy Meal."

—Sidney S. Prasad

Freudian psychologists would refer to this negative behavior as *displacement*, while I would categorize this as needing to have a couple of drinks and get laid once in a while.

To exemplify this, one morning I pulled into the parking lot the same time as Iman S. Hole did. He was pretty warm and cheery as we laughed about the winning goal that won our city the hockey game the night before. Less than two minutes went by and I had barely hung up my coat when I heard, "Sidney, bring your raggedy ass to my desk now!" Thoughts are swimming through my mind like, "Shit, did I park in his spot, or am I going to have to take the rap for the coffee tasting shitty today?"

Iman S. Hole was pissed off because there was no delivery charge on an invoice, and he wanted to know why I missed it. I took a look at the order and said, "What's that special line noting 'delivery charges exempt, as per Iman S. Hole?'"

He apologized and said he was just frustrated because he moved to the suburbs to be close to his best friend. But his so-called best friend's wife wouldn't allow her husband to hang out with him. I'm thinking, this guy actually has friends? I questioned him on how often he saw his best friend. His response was "every two years." I'm thinking, "Okay, this isn't his best friend if he lives in the same city and only hangs out five times per decade."

Perhaps My Bipolar Manager might have accidentally confused the cable guy or his doctor for his best friend. Most bipolar managers are loners because no one wants to be seen in public with them. But still, this was no excuse for My Bipolar Manager to negatively displace his frustrations on me. Fuck, I bet his imaginary friends bailed on him, too.

"Hey did you drop out or get kicked out of anger management class?"

—Sidney S. Prasad

I can appreciate that most managers have to ensure that all of their subordinates execute their duties in accordance with the company norm. But bipolar managers will come out of nowhere and whip themselves into frenzies and get infuriated about the tiniest, miniscule things. It's sort of like a parent giving crap to their kid six months after the Super Bowl for passing them a telemarketing call during the game. I can picture Iman S. Hole giving shit to a baby for not knowing how to walk. It's scary how some people sweat the smallest things in life.

A bipolar manager will never admit when they are wrong, not in a million years. In fact, they would rather lie than admit to their employees they fucked up. One day, Iman S. Hole gave a price override authorization to an intern in our office. Later, the intern named Stella Virgin came back to the office after a meeting with the client quoting the authorized prices. Iman S. Hole realized that he authorized prices below cost. He should have acted like a man and called up the prospect and taken full responsibility for the situation. He instead gloated about the intern getting fired for fucking up. Luckily, I was able to get My Stupid CEO aside and explain the situation and got the poor intern off the hook. I call Izzy Cumming "My Stupid CEO" because he hired My Bipolar Manager.

"Hey, you are supposed to hide behind the police glass and identify your enemy, not join the lineup!"

—Sidney S. Prasad

2 HISTORY OF BIPOLAR MANAGERS

As absurd as this sounds, I have had even nuttier bipolar managers. I have arrived at the conclusion that I attract these weirdoes for some strange reason. I guess there is some validity to the fact that certain people will walk into your life for a very special reason. Some people will stay for an extended period and make your life a living hell — kind of like my nagging girlfriend — while others will come into your life for a brief moment, disguised as waiters or tollbooth operators, just to give you a quick message, leaving you spellbound. You will hold on to those short words for the rest of your life.

I really don't know what the significance was with all the crazy bipolar bosses that I have worked for over the last twenty years. The only thing that I can conclude is to either get hitched to a very wealthy cougar or win the fucken' lottery. After working with a number of maniac managers, I was able to learn two things: The first was to never accept a management position, because there's a slight chance that I might turn into one of those assholes. The second thing was that in the event that I'm stonewalled into accepting a management position, I will do everything in my power to create a positive and nurturing environment. I would reward my employees handsomely for a job well done, and they would love me so much that they would have pictures of me in their homes. Speaking of pictures, I would love to make a roll of toilet paper with all the pictures of my former bipolar managers on it.

"I was curious if My Bipolar Manager could hold a smile for ten seconds in order to take his picture."

—Sidney S. Prasad

I'm going to open the history books and go back in time to my very first bipolar manager. Now, I know it's rocking the boat, but sometimes it is entertaining getting shit from a bipolar manager with a foreign accent. A British or North American accent can sound funny to someone in Zimbabwe. And an East Indian accent would sound interesting to some redneck hick in Texas. I remember my first job working at a pizza parlor when I was thirteen. Not only was my manager, named Pee Don Yu, bipolar, he was also a psycho. He actually looked forward to the day someone would rob him, as he had an arsenal of homemade weapons underneath the cash register. He even kept nunchucks in his car, just in case someone attempted to short-change him during a pizza delivery.

Sometimes when I got bored, I would purposely overcook the odd pizza and hang out with the patrons in the restaurant until I heard the kitchen door slam open. Pee Don Yu would call my name, but he couldn't pronounce "Sidney" with his Asian accent and would call me Silly instead. Then, he would say, "Silly, Silly, you burn pizza, you burn pizza, holy fuck." Then, for the next twenty minutes, he would swear at me in a couple of different dialects. In some sort of sick way, I got a kick out of it. (Please note there is no racism intended to anyone who conveys themselves in a foreign kind of manner.)

"I don't drink, smoke, or gamble, but I am a fucken' chronic pathological liar!"

—Sidney S. Prasad

At some point, we all wish that we were born into a rich, powerful, affluent family with a silver spoon stuck up our ass. We imagine that we would have no problems that our parents' money couldn't solve. We envision how grand life would be, sort of like a constant never-ending party. In fact, we think life would be so awesome that we could afford to waste an extra three years in high school, then spend seven years on a two-year college diploma. During those seven years, we would hit every keg party and all those late-night panty raids. Then, finally, when we're ready for the real world, we would hit our parents up for a new home by the ocean and an executive position in the family business.

Sure, this sounds like the perfect life in a fantasy world, but we are forgetting about one important element: We would be fucken' bored out of our tree. There is only so much booze, drugs, and sex one can have before getting sick of it, right? Well, if that's what you consider fun. But the tabloids and newspapers are full of rich celebrities and their kids who are in and out of rehab.

Being born into a middle-class, low-class or no-class family is a blessing in disguise. It's totally all right if you live in a trailer and eat Kraft dinner every other night. The experiences that we get can be compared to a precious gem. I can tell you there were countless times where I busted a gut laughing so hard in the customer service line up at Walmart. There is always the same scenario where someone is screaming at the top of their lungs in hopes of getting a two-dollar refund without a receipt for some used, soiled underwear. Talk to almost any long-haul truck driver and they will leave you amazed with astonishment about the shit that goes on the road and truck stops.

A waitress or bartender can mesmerize you with the funky things people do when they are drunk. But what stories can a surgeon who earns five hundred thousand per year share with you? Their maids do all their shopping and the only action that they see is at the golf course with their fat-ass buddies in pajama pants.

"Hey guys, please help me carry the boss outside. The sign at the front said to leave your problems at the door!"

—Sidney S. Prasad

Can you picture a lawyer telling you stories about a bipolar judge that they dealt with? Chances are slim and next-to-none, as judges are closely monitored and regulated. But on the other hand, representing the common folks, I can remember my second job working in the kitchen of a high-end restaurant as a salad man & short order cook. The entire shift, my boss Ben Dover kept praising me on doing such a wonderful job. He was so grateful to me for covering a couple of shifts for a sick coworker. Then, in the last hour of the shift, a waiter named Howie Dewett alerted the boss that an irate customer shit all over the outside of the kitchen door. It was the middle of winter and the shit was frozen solid to the metal door. Ben Dover asked me to get a mop and boiling hot water and clean it up. I was pretty insulted and felt Howie Dewett should have received the shitty assignment, considering it was his shitty discovery.

Silly me wasn't aware that Ben Dover was a bipolar manager, considering that he was praising me for the last six hours. As a joke, I took the poopy mop to his face and said, "Hey, Ben Dover, is this shit?" He didn't answer and went inside the restaurant. When I finished cleaning the shit for my shitty boss, I went back inside the kitchen. Ben Dover greeted me and handed me two envelopes. The first envelope had a final paycheck, and the second envelope had an employment separation slip marked "laid off." I asked the head chef, Dan Singh, "What does 'laid off' mean?" He explained to me that it's a nice way of saying "fuck off!" In a way, I was glad that I saw my manager's true bipolar colors and discovered how fucken' anal he was over a little shit — literally.

"I will leave you alone and let you talk amongst yourself!"

—Sidney S. Prasad

A wise man once told me that the only reason that anyone in society had a job is because someone else couldn't handle the boss's shit and jumped ship, which led to the vacancy. As strange as that sounds, it made complete sense to me. I truly believe that the universe has a strange way of unfolding. There might not be any logic whatsoever to how we attract events and circumstances in our life. I justify all the weird bipolar managers that I have attracted into my life were clearly brought in for a reason. That reason was so I can make fun of them behind their backs, have some outrageously funny drinking stories, and publish a couple of dry-humored books about their craziness.

In my senior year of high school, I worked for a restaurant as a busboy. That's where I initially picked up a lot of life experience about people in general. Graveyard shifts were amazing because you got the clubbing crowd, bikers, policemen, punk rockers, and a really well behaved group of transvestites. For the most part, at a macro level, all those personality types were completely sane in my eyes compared to My Bipolar Manager, Hugh Jass. I heard a lot of stories about Hugh Jass but had never really made it into his bad books.

"Karma is a bitch! I'm curious on what I did in my last life to be punished working for this asshole?"

—Sidney S. Prasad

There was this one busboy named Sal Ladd who was notorious for not cleaning the entire dish rack before the end of his shift, which was a mandatory requirement as per company regulations. All the other busboys on the night shift complained, but nothing got done. So my busboy colleague Myles Long and I took it upon ourselves to get this guy fired.

Myles Long got a garbage bag and filled it up with dirty pots and pans. Then, conveniently, my partner in crime reported it to My Bipolar Manager Hugh Jass, blaming Sal Ladd. I'm not sure what happened, but two minutes later, I was called into the office and was fired on the spot. I wasn't really too worried, as I was going to quit my job once I began college in the fall to study gynecology.

Within an hour, I got home and, magically, the phone rang. Hugh Jass apologized to me, said he had a rough week, and rehired me with a raise and promotion. I gladly accepted the promotion and was back to work the next day.

There definitely is a God! Because within a week, the entire wait staff approached the regional manager and said that they were going to walk out unless Hugh Jass was fired. Apparently Hugh Jass had a history of mood swings, boinking waitresses, and even stealing money from the tip jar.

"I'm from planet earth. Where are you from?"

—Sidney S. Prasad

Are you beginning to see an emerging pattern with all these managers so far? It's fair to agree that these guys can change their moods faster than I can flip my underwear. Most people don't floor their gas pedal when pulling out of their driveway.

At the same token, it gradually takes a while for a sane person to get pissed off and do something they will regret later. A few years later, while working in the corporate world as a marketing coordinator for a luxury cruise company, I got the privilege of understanding the mechanics of playing a mental tennis game with a lunatic bipolar manager.

At 1:00 PM, My Bipolar Manager named Willie Dewer came into my office and, out of the blue, told me that I was fired. His basis was that I blew my marketing budget and my sales were low. My response was that I understand and respected his opinion. He then asked me why I repeatedly attempted to get a meeting with him during the last ninety days. My response was that I was trying to inform him that the big three auto manufacturers might be potentially going under unless they get a bailout loan from Washington. Therefore, it wasn't wise for me to be advertising to all the automobile dealers across America. Willie Dewer told me that that was a valid point; I'm thinking, how the hell anyone on this planet cannot know this? Willie Dewer told me that it didn't matter now, as I was fired, and he left my office. I attempted to squeeze my butt cheeks really hard, but was unsuccessful in letting out a big, juicy, get-the-fuck-out-of-my-office fart.

At that point in my life I felt pretty confident and savvy when dealing with bipolar managers. So I kept working away calling up car dealerships and sending out care packages. At 3:00 PM Willie Dewer came back to my office and questioned me on why I was still there. I told him that I am technically still at his disposal till 4:30 PM and don't want to be insubordinate in fulfilling my contractual obligations. He was really touched by my speech and rehired me within a minute of that statement. I then responded by thanking him and told him where to shove his job . Then I walked out with my nose up in air and a big smile on my kisser. Sure he owns a boat, fancy cars and a nice home but that satisfaction was priceless.

3 WHAT PLANET ARE THEY FROM?

After traveling down memory lane learning about My Bipolar Managers from the early days, let me ask you a couple of questions: Have you ever questioned the mortal status of your bipolar manager? Might their erratic, irrational behaviors and inhumane treatment of people be a hint that they are from a galaxy far, far away?

I bring this up because most people communicate quite rationally with their colleagues in both good and bad situations. But for a manager to blow a gasket and bark at their subordinates like a Pit bull makes me wonder if My Bipolar Manager is even human.

What do these maniacs eat to get so damn hyperactive? Most people are like zombies during the first couple hours of their day until they have had a couple cups of coffee. Even then, it takes us till about 11:00 AM to start functioning at a normal consciousness level. But bipolar managers are similar to hyperactive three-year-olds buzzing off grape soda, regardless of what time of day it is. Iman S. Hole wouldn't hesitate to swear at someone at the top of his lungs during the first few minutes of his shift. When he would come towards our desk ready to unload, it would remind me of a NHL hockey player getting out of the penalty box, ready to kill.

"It's Happy Hour, not Happy Minute. Are you sure you can last?"

—Sidney S. Prasad

There are several people who just love to dive into Cajun food. Some of these people even add gobs of hot sauce and eat it like a salad. It's safe to say that their tolerance allows them to eat the most exotic peppers on the planet on a normal, habitual basis. But on the flip side, we have witnessed people take a bite out of a hot wing that then causes their face to instantly turn red and drip with sweat.

I use this analogy to describe how fast Iman S. Hole would whip himself into a frenzy. One day, Eileen Dover and I were talking about these two guys who won the state lottery. Within thirty seconds, we looked over our shoulders to discover Iman S. Hole, who was redder than a California tomato. It certainly didn't help that he was a bald Caucasian, because the vein on top of his head was throbbing like the dink of a male who just lost his virginity.

He escorted us to the boardroom and gave us a lecture about inappropriate conversations at the workplace. We were thinking, what the fuck did we do so wrong for discussing the latest lottery winners? Apparently, he thought we were gay-bashing, because the two gentlemen who won the lottery were a gay couple. Our reaction was dumbfounded, as we had no idea of the sexual orientation of the couple and it really didn't matter to us if they were gay or straight. To make the situation worse, I asked My Bipolar Manager sarcastically if gay people were allowed to play the state lottery. I got sent home early with no pay.

Eileen Dover went back to her desk and proceeded with her work. Ten minutes later, Iman S. Hole demonstrated his bipolar mood swings by pretending like nothing had happened and presented Eileen Dover with a lottery ticket that he had bought for her.

"If we are what we eat, then my boss must be a carnivore, because he is the biggest meathead!"

—Sidney S. Prasad

On occasion, our company would rent out a private section of a two-star restaurant for quarterly meetings. We were forced to carpool, and I got stuck with my head purchaser, Pu Ping, and My Bipolar Manager. Ironically, in order to get to the restaurant, we had to pass a maximum-security mental hospital. I couldn't let that opportunity pass, and I'm like, "Pu Ping, stop the car and let Iman S. Hole off."

You probably have a good idea what happened next. For the duration of the trip, My Bipolar Manager gave me bucket loads of shit about insinuating that he had a mental disability. I knew that I wasn't insinuating it because it was the plain truth.

We finally arrived at the dive restaurant and My Stupid CEO, Izzy Cumming, decided to splurge by ordering five appetizers for forty people. He expected us to feed off the snack trays like vultures fighting for bread. I personally am a germaphobe and can confirm that half of my colleagues don't wash their hands after they take a big, fat, mango-sized shit. While my co-workers raped the snack trays like it was their last supper, I sat in a corner with a glass of water. It's amazing how people who don't wash their hands love to lick their fingers when they eat.

"Order your date fish and you fed her for the night. Teach her how to fish and you're not getting laid!"

—Sidney S. Prasad

Iman S. Hole came up to me and sympathetically asked why I wasn't eating. It's like he totally forgot about the abusive car ride and was suddenly concerned for my well-being. I replied by telling him that I saw Gabe Oy scratching his balls at work, so that eliminates the nachos. Winnie Bago uses her hands as a Kleenex and that eliminated the fried zucchini sticks and onion rings. The other two dishes have meat in them, and I'm a vegan. Quite frankly, if I did eat meat, I wouldn't go near those two meat platters anyways. This was because the office slut, Liz Bien, was doing something obscene with one of the warehouse guys during her lunch break. So it kind of sickens me to watch her snacking on the meat trays with her stinky dinky fingers. God only knows what types of diseases that she was hosting.

26

Iman S. Hole told me that he totally understood my situation and not to worry. He then handed me a menu and told me to order whatever I wanted, on him. I was blown away that the guy who just gave me shit doesn't want me to go hungry and was buying me a special dinner.

If you people watch and observe human behavior, then I am confident that you would agree that it takes a while for people to shift their behavioral gears. For example, if someone just got into an extremely vocal shouting match, then they usually need a walk or to wait a couple of hours till they cool down. Even a screaming baby takes a while to adjust before they calm down. This is clearly because we are all normal, breathing, and functional human beings. I still can't fathom how My Bipolar Manager could be unrealistically irate one minute and then be all cheery and smiley the next minute.

"You got to be pretty fucken' stupid to mug someone on a airplane."

—Sidney S. Prasad

4 YOU'RE AS GOOD AS YOUR LAST SALE

For those readers who have never worked in a sales environment before, let me tell you that sales managers are the most notorious candidates for acting bipolar. They are your best friends when you are breaking sales records and your worst enemies on your drought days. It's like going to a restaurant and listening to some lard-ass hassle the poor waiter about the whereabouts of his dinner. All of a sudden, the kitchen door swings open and the food arrives. Then the fat slob is like the nicest and bubbliest guy in the restaurant.

In the world of selling, salesmen are forced to adapt to the philosophy of being as good as their last sale. For example, commissioned salespeople wake up every morning unemployed. The sales manager gives no mercy and won't take any prisoners. I remember working in this one "boiler room" and got stuck with a steroid-monkey sales manager named Max E. Padd. He was really outgoing at times and the coolest guy to party with. However, when the sales were low, Max E. Padd would rip us a new asshole. He would even put McDonald's application forms on our desk. Max E. Padd would boldly tell us that if we wanted to keep our seat on his team, then start making some sales or go flip some burgers. I didn't want to fuck with this guy so magically I always made my quota.

"Life is tough, especially when your boss is a lazy Nazi!"

—Sidney S. Prasad

One factor that attributes to sales managers' radical change in behavior is that they usually get a cut of their agents' commissions. It's like the telemarketer is the call girl and the sales manager is their pimp. I strongly believe if someone is going to take a cut of my poverty-level wages then I am going to make them work for it. Iman S. Hole was the weakest sales manager that I have ever worked for. In fact, he carried himself like a floppy penis, with not a shred of confidence.

My colleagues and I knew exactly how to activate his bipolar switch. All we would have to say is that a customer is requesting to speak to a manager. I thought, well, hey, if this fucker is earning coin off our sales, then do our dirty work for us!

It was obvious Iman S. Hole didn't have a clue on how to manage a sales team. To be honest with you, I didn't think My Bipolar Manager guy could manage a broom closet without screwing up. Iman S. Hole was so stupid he could fuck up a cup of black coffee.

Our sales day would begin at 8:00 AM and end at 3:30 PM. My Bipolar Manager's strategy was to post the updated sales figures at 11:00 AM, and then again at 1:30 PM. Then, around 3:00 PM, he would get up our ass like a swollen hemorrhoid to sell our hearts out. Most successful sales managers will push their reps to make their daily quota as early as possible and then half the pressure is eliminated. This makes perfect sense, right? It's like, do the hardest task first, such as working out at 5:00 AM, and then rest of the day will go by smoothly.

"To meditate is to be one with the universe, and to masturbate is being one with yourself."

—Sidney S. Prasad

No matter how I put it, Iman S. Hole needed to get his head examined, as we couldn't have a day without him pulling a bipolar episode. The one thing my colleagues and I could do was try to minimize the bipolar episodes. So, I took it upon myself to email My Stupid CEO, Izzy Cumming, and explain the situation. I also offered a solution, which was for Iman S. Hole to announce the sales figures every half-hour between 8:00 AM and 3:00 PM. This way, the telephone hookers could monitor their own sales and we wouldn't have to witness My Bipolar Manager's 3:00 PM temper tantrums.

My Stupid CEO responded to my email by placing Iman S. Hole and me into a closed boardroom meeting. Iman S. Hole confronted me about criticizing his management style. I had to choose my words carefully, because I was in a closed boardroom with a psycho. Based on my personal experience with bipolar managers, I was pretty confident that I could calm this fucker down by fucking with his cherry-size brain.

I opened the blinds and asked him to look at the sky. I then asked him if he noticed the clouds in the sky. He responded that he saw the clouds, but didn't know how that related to me going over his bald head. I told him everything and nothing! He then immediately requested that I elaborate on that statement. That's when I knew I had him by his itchy balls. I proceeded to tell him that he could hypothesize that the cloud on the left looks like a cat and I can hypothesize the cloud on the right looks like a dog. Either way, we are both equally right and equally wrong, therefore there are no winners or losers.

"Where did you escape from? Oops, Freudian slip of the tongue — I meant to ask you where you were from."

—Sidney S. Prasad

The strategy that I used was interrupting his mental pattern and scratching the record inside his head. I then asked if he could explain in detail how the engine in his car runs. Then, if he could offer an explanation, would his mechanical philosophy be accepted by most mainstream mechanics today?

Iman S. Hole responded by telling me that he didn't know what type of game I was playing, and he forgot why we were in this closed-door meeting. He ended the meeting by instructing me to go back to my desk and make some sales. One of the best ways to deal with insane managers in those sorts of situations is just ask a question that is completely random or the polar opposite to the question presented. Eventually, your nutjob boss will think you're bonkers, and then you've won the game.

The sad reality is there is no exact science to the madness that drives bipolar managers. Basically, Iman S. Hole would love you after you closed a big fat thousand-dollar sale. But if that's the only sale you made, then two hours later he would automatically switch into bipolar mode, in which he would kick you in the ass and leave his footprint for your colleagues to see. Iman S. Hole was the type of guy who would recognize the sales superstar from the previous day and personally thank them for their valuable contribution. Ten minutes later, if the sales representative had only made some small sales, he would then be on them like flies on an outhouse till the end of the day.

Most bipolar managers are pretty ignorant and fail to recognize that the employees that they badger cannot function properly. This is because after they have humiliated their employees, their employees' self-esteem has been bruised and they are put into a fight-or-flight situation.

"If an employee can take a mental health day off, then can a bipolar manager take a mental health year off?"

—Sidney S. Prasad

It's common to have a sales cycle that runs for ninety days. Judgment Day, or the end of the sales cycle, is always an interesting event with colorful repercussions. At that moment in time, the bipolar manager is supposed to have a little sit-down with the sales representatives. Normally, these meetings go only two ways. The telephone hooker could get their ass ripped apart royally in there, followed by a bunch of accusations on why their bipolar manager thinks they aren't think they are producing. The sales representative cannot dare to blame the bipolar manager's negativity and absurd behavior for their sales slump, or they will get fired. The other direction for this meeting is kind words of praise by the impressed bipolar manager, followed by a pat on the bum.

The true bipolar colors come out during the end of the sales cycle. One day, my co-worker Yora Hogg was in one of those meetings. When they came out, Iman S. Hole was preaching about what a model employee she was, exceeding her quota by thirty percent. Obviously, he was happy because he got a huge bonus for pimping her, even though Yora Hogg's sales were purely based on her own hard work. Sure, let Iman S. Hole gloat, I thought. He is probably going to the strip club after work and getting a lap dance from a tranny stripper with his newly found cash.

Yora Hogg had her own little celebration after work with a crazy night of Monopoly and Charades. I wasn't sure why she was hung over the next morning, because she doesn't really drink alcohol. Yora Hogg was the type of chick who served Kool-Aid at her parties. Her sales were quite low the following day, and sure enough Iman S. Hole pulled her into the boardroom three times during that shift.

My Bipolar Manager yelled at Yora Hogg at the top of his lungs each time for slacking. She tried to justify her slump by saying that she used all her sales in the bank to top up her sales cycle that ended yesterday. This was a common strategy among salespeople. Iman S. Hole claimed that wasn't a valid reason and sent her home for being insubordinate.

"I asked My Stupid CEO to ask My Bipolar Manager to pretend to be normal for eight hours!"

—Sidney S. Prasad

I find it really amazing how soon bipolar managers forget the successes of yesterday. It is like instant fucken' amnesia or something. I can only guess that in the bipolar management world, the word "consistency" doesn't exist. One day, Iman S. Hole was on top of the world because he felt like a Mack Daddy for picking up some female of barely legal age on an online dating website. He even called me to his desk to show me this chick's picture on his cell phone. I swear, this was one of the ugliest-looking mutants I had ever have seen. I was quite confident that he was paying her to talk to him or something.

Anyway, it was nice to see a smile on his face. Then, my colleague Sheeza Freak announced that Penny Less Incorporated was returning three thousand dollars worth of unused product. Holy fuck. Iman S. Hole instantly started acting like a stockbroker during the crash of 1929. The remainder of the shift, he bitched all of his subordinates out, one by one. I got sent home for rolling my eyes at him. He personally did me a favor, though, as it was a hot day and I wanted to go to the nude beach and make fun of the old people sun tanning there.

"I noticed on your online dating profile, under the subject heading, 'personality,' you put 'multiple.'"

—Sidney S. Prasad

5 CAN A NUT SELL ICE TO AN ESKIMO?

During my childhood, I had the opportunity to embark on karate lessons and learn the skills of martial arts. One summer, my karate class went out to the Rocky Mountains of Alberta for a special training camp. My karate master shared a really interesting story with us that can be applied to almost any profession.

He told us about this little island somewhere in the Pacific. Apparently, there was a large mountain at the center of the island. The grandmaster, who was the most talented and toughest competitor, lived at the top of the mountain. Imagine that from the moment that you arrive on the shore of the island, there would be amateur karate athletes guarding the perimeter. Then, as you slowly start winding up the mountain, the more novice karate competitors there would be. As you start to reach the top of the mountain, you would be face-to-face with the most advanced karate experts. If, by some fluke, you succeeded in making past the advanced athletes, then you would get the opportunity to challenge the grandmaster to a match.

"Does the freedom of speech charter apply to the dialogue of insane managers?"

—Sidney S. Prasad

I truly believe this model should be applied to the model of selling and any other field. Wouldn't you agree that the savviest and sharpest people, who have mastered the craft, should earn the manager's title? A popular movie back in the day was *Glengarry Glen Ross*, with Al Pacino and Alec Baldwin. There was a famous sales-meeting scene where Alec Baldwin, as the most polished salesman, motivated the deadbeat slacking salesmen. My Stupid CEO should have adopted that model and incorporated it into his company. This way, the legitimate role models with proven track records would sit at the top.

In the movie *Boiler Room*, there was a famous scene with Vin Diesel. The scene entailed a hesitant doctor talking to a rookie broker. Then, Vin Diesel took over the call and closed the doctor on the spot for two thousand shares of stock. I can't tell you how many times I've thought about that scene.

The truth of the matter is Iman S. Hole couldn't sell shit to a toilet paper factory if his life depended on it. Naturally, I figured the title "sales manager" was reserved as a promotion for the sharpest salesman or woman in the boiler room. I also thought that should have been the deciding factor by My Stupid CEO, Izzy Cumming, to hire anyone in his position. Unfortunately, My Stupid CEO fluked out and never had a fucken' job in his entire lifetime.

In my personal opinion, there are two types of people in business: The entrepreneurs who have made it to where they are today with sheer talent, goals, and hard work. Then there are those rare exceptions of people, who fluked out and were at the right place at the right time to make it big. My Stupid CEO fell into the fluke category.

I challenge my readers to think about the six people that you commonly spend the most time with. Then, on a piece of paper, list their incomes. If you add up all six incomes and divide it by six, you will arrive at your salary. It's the law of averages.

A long time ago, a couple of famous authors approached Anthony Robbins and complained that they were sick of earning ten to thirty million dollars per year. They wanted to get into the hundred-million income bracket. Anthony Robbins asked them to carefully examine who they hung out with and suggested that they find some friends and role models who were already in the hundred-million dollar range. Sure enough, they succeeded with their goal and eventually achieved it.

When interviewing for a position, I always try to pick the brain of my prospective CEO and ask which companies they have worked for and their positions. Also, I check the earnings of the company. If I am going to commit to working for anyone, I want to rub shoulders with the best.

"If I had to lie through my teeth to get a job working for My Bipolar Manager, then what the fuck did he have to do to get his job?"

—Sidney S. Prasad

Based on My Stupid CEO's company track record, and the large well-known corporations that Iman S. Hole previously worked for, I strongly felt I was surrounding myself with champions. Boy, what a crock of shit that was, as they both bamboozled me royally.

Early in my career working for Iman S. Hole, I learned really fast that he had no sales ability whatsoever. What's even worse that is he was an idea and story stealer. Every morning, we would have a sales meeting and all the sales representatives would have to share a story from the previous day. The story would be based on a negative client experience and how we turned it around, or a positive client story on how we upsold a client and made them a lifelong customer. Iman S. Hole would carefully pay close attention to what we said, word for word. Then, a week later, he would try to feed our words right back to us and pretend they were his experiences when he was a salesperson. This is how he felt eruditely wise in his sick little mind. This was pure insanity, as we had witnesses that these were our original sales stories. Now there was a charlatan taking credit for our stories and preaching it like it was his own tale.

"We lost the game because the cheerleaders were bipolar."

—Sidney S. Prasad

To take it a step further, whenever My Stupid CEO or one of his suit dummy executives were present, My Bipolar Manager would spread the bullshit even deeper. They all thought he was brilliant and innovatively creative based on his stolen stories and ideas. To date, he was the weakest manager and human being that I have ever met. Not only was he a drain on our entire staff, but we had to carry his ass throughout the duration of his time with the company. As mentioned before, he was sort of like our pimp and we were the telephone prostitutes bringing millions of dollars to the company. My Bipolar Manager, Iman S. Hole, earned commissions and bonuses based on our sales, blood, sweat, and tears. I loved making Iman S. Hole shit out chunks and make him work for the money. Like I mentioned earlier all it took to ruin the guy's day was to tell him that a customer was holding to speak to the manager.

"I could eat alphabet cereal and puke out a better sales pitch!"

—Sidney S. Prasad

I decided to fuck him over really hard one day with an attempt to expose him as a fraud. Our outside sales manager, Wilma Dickfit, quit shortly after she discovered Iman S. Hole was a bipolar manager. We had no one representing those of us out in the trenches with her departure. I waited till we were short-staffed inside, as two other sales executives were on vacation. Then, I scheduled a meeting with a large potential account and requested that My Stupid CEO and Iman S. Hole represent me. They both agreed and proceeded with the meeting. The next day, My Stupid CEO told us that he thought it was kind of cute that My Bipolar Manager was scared to go into the sales meeting. Iman S. Hole blatantly told My Stupid CEO, Izzy Cumming, that he wasn't sure how to conduct himself in a sales meeting. Now if you were a CEO or Iman S. Hole's boss, wouldn't you question his salesmanship and the rest of the rhetoric on his resume at that point? Unfortunately, My Stupid CEO didn't consider that a red flag. My little plan failed miserably.

"The Human Resources Department wants the name and phone number of your shrink in case of an emergency."

—Sidney S. Prasad

The company that we worked for was a dot-com company with no showroom. We had a tiny office and a little warehouse. On the odd occasion, we would have customers walk in and attempt to purchase something they saw online. Whenever any of my colleagues or I would hear someone come in the office and start asking questions, we would pick up our phones and make outgoing calls. This would force Iman S. Hole to deal with the customer. On about two occasions, maybe, he successfully sold a ten-dollar item after a thirty-minute presentation. In comparison, the sales executives could close a five-thousand-dollar deal in that same time frame. Iman S. Hole didn't catch on that we were making a fool out of him, forcing him to sell. However, he was a lazy Nazi and enjoyed sitting on his rump while hitting on young chicks on Internet dating websites. (He might have been hitting on little boys too, but I haven't dared to confirm that yet.)

After about three presentations over a period of six months, Iman S. Hole appointed someone to help anyone that walked into the office. Maybe he caught on that he was the inside joke of the office.

"One who is at bliss with the creator will come across crazy to an insane man. However, one who is in denial of the creator will appear insane to the spiritual man!"

—Sidney S. Prasad

I arrived at the conclusion that I was in a desperate situation when applying for this position and had to take whatever was offered to me. After this experience with My Bipolar Manager, I promised myself to do a point check with my next prospective sales manager. Iman S. Hole was lacking quite a few qualities that champion sales managers exude. A professional sales manager will be conservatively dressed to the nines. Iman S. Hole's attire would include something too loose on the top and something really tight on the bottom. A well-polished veteran sales manager will have the firmest handshake. Iman S. Hole had a sweaty handshake, like he had just finished jacking off in the broom closet. An advanced and experienced sales manager will have a ton of energy, full of enthusiasm. Iman S. Hole always seemed like he just came back from a funeral, as he was tapped out of energy from shitting on his staff. There is a high level of confidence and magnetism among top sales managers. Iman S. Hole was like a big floppy cock with no confidence whatsoever.

"If it's an eye for an eye, and your psycho boss rats you out for being tardy, then you aren't doing any justice for not reporting him to the authorities for being mentally challenged."

—Sidney S. Prasad

Speaking of confidence, our office was located next to a well-known casino. I remember telling Iman S. Hole that sometimes I would go in there and hit on random women and see how many phone numbers I could score. I explained to him that it was how I would keep my confidence level in check for approaching new clients. He told me that he was too scared to approach women and did not have the personality to execute such a daring move. I was astonished how a veteran sales manger could be this shy. This was because most sales professionals will just "fake it till they make it" and pretend that they have confidence.

"My Stupid CEO thought a Porsche 911 was a police car."

—Sidney S. Prasad, My Stupid CEO

6 POWER TRIP

How many times have you heard your bipolar manager use the following phrases?

- "I want you to come to my desk right now!"
- "I want you to do it now!"
- "I don't care!"
- "I am the boss!"
- "I make the final call!"
- "I will decide that!"
- "I am annoyed!"
- "Because I said so!"

There is one common word with these statements, and that's "I."

Power-tripping bipolar managers love to flex their occupational muscles and bully their employees. In the field of selling, sales representatives are taught that everybody's favorite radio station is **WII-FM**, which stands for, **W**HAT'S **I**N **I**T **F**OR **M**E? Iman S. Hole's favorite words included I, MY, and ME.

"Is being abnormal normal for you?"

—Sidney S. Prasad

At some point in our lives, our ears have heard the heavenly sounds of musicians playing instruments passionately. That sound was so sweet, like it was their calling in life to play those notes. That is similar to our taste buds being fed food like it was made in God's kitchen. There is a good chance the chef was working in his or her chosen field of endeavor.

However, I have always felt that Iman S. Hole was like the biggest loser of his high school. His main purpose in becoming a manager was retribution and getting even with everyone that ever picked on him. He accomplished this daily by making every single one of his employees' lives hell.

Most people who have been in the workforce for a few years usually have a pretty good idea of the do's and don'ts of the workplace. Iman S. Hole had a surefire strategy in his sick little mind. Other than myself, who he hired to be his personal Google-like search engine to lean on for sales and marketing strategies, Iman S. Hole would only hire very young females between nineteen and twenty-three years of age. He hypothesized that if someone was younger, then they would be light-years dumber than him. At the same time, Iman S. Hole would concentrate on chasing people over the age of twenty-three out of the company. Most power-tripping managers live under a false assumption that people respect their elders. Respect is something that is earned for all ages across the board.

"Good morning, sir. How are you doing today? I will check back in two minutes to see how you are doing again."

—Sidney S. Prasad

Iman S. Hole thought that he was razor-sharp by dishing out shit and serving it on a platter wherever he spotted a flaw in something or someone. He was such a nut that we would have to take extra-special steps to deliver everything down to a T. God forbid if Iman S. Hole caught us wiping our ass the wrong way. In his dimension, he came from a school of management that gave out orders by barking like a Pit bull.

There are two types of bipolar managers. One is the sort of lunatic that gives shit to their employees and vents their personal anger as a therapeutic outlet. The second kind of bipolar manager gives shit to people because they get a rush out of watching their employees shit their pants. Fuck, after two weeks working for this guy, I treated everyone to some adult diapers. Sadly enough, Iman S. Hole was an exception to the rule and fit into *both* categories.

Part of My Bipolar Manager's craziness was in finding creative ways to infuriate his employees. One of his techniques would be to accuse us of being insubordinate in not completing assignments that he clearly didn't assign. Like this one time he went out on a tangent on Eileen Dover and me for being tardy in handing in some reports on floor-cleaning products. Iman S. Hole claimed to have assigned this to us on Friday. Eileen Dover and I attempted to defend ourselves, responding by saying that new software had been installed on the weekend. Therefore, we had no training on it and wouldn't be able to run reports. For some strange reason, he wouldn't accept that as a valid answer. I then decided to launch a nuclear missile and say, "Come to think of it, you weren't even here on Friday, so how could you assign this to us?"

"I am going to the mental asylum, because My Bipolar Manger told me to put myself in his shoes."

—Sidney S. Prasad

Some may speculate that this was career suicide, but who gives a shit? I thought, at worst, I get fired and go out in style. Iman S. Hole pulled me into the boardroom and started ranting on me for not respecting the chain of command. I absorbed all his negativity and then calmly told him the following statement: "I have been in the field of selling for a long time and can read people like a book. Please take a breather and we can discuss this when you are calm."

He responded, "I am calm, and how do you know how I am feeling?" I told him that it was written all over his body language, complemented by his crossed arms. This caused him to start hesitating; he was desperate for a comeback. Then, like usual, he fed my words back to me and told me that he could read my body language, which showed anger. I laughed at him, and said; "You are on some power trip, eh?"

He then changed the topic, and for the next ten minutes, I played a mental manipulation game with him. Every time he would ask me a question, I would respond with a fucked-up analogy. After each analogy, I would nod, as nodding is contagious — that's an old salesman trick. This would cause him to nod, and I would say, "Great. Now explain this to me, since you nodded."

He was so dumbfounded and couldn't fight his way out of the conversation. I ended up getting sent home without pay for being a smart-ass. I laughed the whole way home, because it was blatantly obvious that he had no valid basis for sending me home other than flexing his bipolar management muscles.

"My psycho boss is stuck to me like Krazy Glue!"

—Sidney S. Prasad

I'm about to make a profound statement, so I must warn you in advance! The only thing worse thing than a bipolar manager is a bipolar manager with seniority.

There was another bald fucker called Ray Pist who was the senior logistics manager. He had been in the company for eons and should have been locked up in a mental hospital a long time ago. Apparently, rumor had it that he used to be an elementary school teacher and messed up. I never confirmed it, but was curious if maybe it wasn't an elementary school that he got fired from, because I can totally see him mismanaging a day-care. Plus he looked like a freak and fit the profile of a weirdo.

Iman S. Hole and Ray Pist were at war since the day Iman S. Hole signed into the company. They were both bipolar, they were both bald, and they were both power-hungry. This was one of the only people that Iman S. Hole couldn't scare off, as Ray Pist was ten years older than him. Both of them had the same twisted strategy of sticking it to each other by putting sanctions on the other person's departmental employees. So the first sanction from Ray Pist was that all the sales executives were restricted from talking to him from between the times of 3:30 PM and 4:30 PM because it was critical crunch time. More like his critical ball-scratching time. Then, Iman S. Hole retaliated by writing a complaint letter to My Stupid CEO. The letter stated that Ray Pist's employees squandered their time talking to the sales staff when they were coming and going from the shitter. "Where's the fucken' toilet paper?" doesn't constitute as a long conversation in my book.

"You are the boss and your job is fucking up. I'm your employee and my job is cleaning up your fuck-ups!"

—Sidney S. Prasad

The war continued as Ray Pist made a beef that the salespeople were doing personal shit on their computers. We won that one, as we explained to My Stupid CEO that watching YouTube videos prior to our shifts and during our breaks should be acceptable. Ray Pist dropped a bomb on Iman S. Hole by banning all sales staff in the perimeter of the warehouse.

Iman S. Hole stole his idea, and then convinced My Stupid CEO, Izzy Cumming, that all of Ray Pist's staff weren't allowed to talk to the sales staff. The only communication they could have is relaying their concerns to Iman S. Hole, who would pass it over to the sales staff. Is this the Mafia? Because that's how mob bosses received their messages.

Iman S. Hole had another target in our office, and that was single moms. He figured he could shit all over them because they needed the money and wouldn't quit so easy. Iman S. Hole marched into Pu Ping's office and dumped a pile of papers on her desk. He then shouted at her, demanded she take care of whatever was on the papers, and proceeded back to his desk.

Pu Ping ran out of her office and threw the papers on the floor and humiliated Iman S. Hole in front of the entire office. She told him that she was tired of his shit and wouldn't tolerate his childish behavior. This was a glorious day because she squashed him right in front of our eyes like a helpless ant. To add the icing on the cake, she filed a complaint immediately afterward with our vice president regarding Iman S. Hole's relentless behavior. When she got back to her office, I slipped her a note and volunteered to be a witness against My Bipolar Manager, as I wanted a piece of the action too!

"You could spend $100 an hour on a therapist to make you feel good. Or you could spend $20 at Happy Hour and you will feel better!"

—Sidney S. Prasad

7 THE ART OF EAVESDROPPING

Regardless of what walk of life you come from or your personal background, we can all agree that nobody appreciates an eavesdropper. Yet anyone who has ever stated that their manager is bipolar usually also adds that their manager has supersonic hearing.

Whether I was in the lunchroom discussing some raunchy shit about my date on Friday night or I was in a colleague's office, Iman S. Hole would always manage to stick his snout where it didn't belong. Fuck, even outside the workplace he would manage to have his way of eavesdropping on my conversations.

I really don't know the root cause behind why Iman S. Hole wanted to live vicariously through his staff. His eavesdropping addiction could be attributed to his life being so lame. All of us in the office felt the guy had no life outside of work. Maybe he didn't own a television either, and we were his only form of entertainment. Fuck, I wish he would just take a look in the mirror and get a good laugh once in a while.

The odd time when I would be on the train commuting to work or shopping, I would hear the raunchiest shit. I tried my best to block it out, as I wanted to give that same respect to the stranger who was gabbing away about the hot apple pie that they experimented with. Kind of like if my girlfriend started giving me shit for sleeping with her friends again. I wouldn't want that to be public knowledge. Or at least until I blogged about it.

"Just because the world is going crazy, why buy into the peer pressure?"

—Sidney S. Prasad

Geographically, Iman S. Hole's desk was at least seventy-five feet from Joe King's accounting office. I remember one day I went in there to give him a heads-up about turning off a client's credit because they kept defaulting on paying for their toilet paper. When I left my desk, Iman S. Hole was sitting comfortably behind his desk touching himself. I didn't even see him get up or hear his footsteps behind me on the way to Joe King's office.

After I finished explaining the deadbeat situation to Joe King, I attempted to scratch my ear. I felt my elbow go into someone's flabs-of-steel stomach. It wasn't a six-pack; definitely a keg. Sure enough, it was Iman S. Hole, standing behind me like a shadow. He then escorted me to my desk and gave me shit for not bringing him into the loop about this, even though it wasn't in his domain of duties. I tuned out the shit he was giving me because I still couldn't figure out how he got behind me so fast. I imagined him using the Star Trek transporter. That would be the only scientific explanation to the scenario.

Iman S. Hole had no sense of humor and couldn't handle that I was sort of like the office clown. I took it upon myself to make people laugh whenever I had a chance. But it's like Iman S. Hole only wanted people to laugh at his jokes. First of all, he is a walking comedian, because you just have to look at him and you will laugh.

He started cracking down on me any time he heard anyone laugh in the office. This led me to get technically savvy with my joke telling. Sometimes, I would deliver my jokes via text message, and other times via email. Believe it or not, sometimes we would resort to passing notes to each other to avoid his eavesdropping.

One day, Iman S. Hole had this program installed on our computers that centered on yellow stickies. It was the same concept as an instant messenger, so we could send messages to each other internally within the office. Prior to installing the sticky program, he mentioned he would have access to our conversations if he wanted to monitor them. Most of us couldn't really be bothered knowing that tidbit of information. We figured being an office manager, he would have better things to do with his fucken' time.

Boy, were we wrong about this Nazi! I had a conversation with my client, Anna Conda, who was a big player purchaser. I sold her on buying two thousand dollars' worth of toilet bowl cleaner.

"I'm not crazy, but I'm excessively eccentric!"

—Sidney S. Prasad

Iman S. Hole overheard my conversation and decided to shove his two-inch leprechaun cock into the situation. He rushed to my desk and suggested that I offer another toilet bowl cleaner that he picked. I tried to explain to him that I already checked with our purchasing manager, Pu Ping, a couple days before. I also attempted to squeeze in another sentence, saying that Pu Ping reviewed my product selection and said it was a perfect product for that particular client.

Iman S. Hole then barged into Pu Ping's office and demanded she get off the phone and waste a half-hour of her time regarding this product. She reiterated the exact same thing I told him. Iman S. Hole came back to my desk and apologized and said to go ahead with the deal.

"I can honestly tell you that I didn't do it. It was my other personality's fault."

—Sidney S. Prasad

If My Bipolar Manager had a brain bigger than his two-inch pee-pee, then he could have easily avoided this situation by simply cross-referencing the cost price of both products. Pretty simple in a sane man's world, right? My colleague, Eileen Dover, sent me a sticky asking me what the commotion was about. I told her that Iman S. Hole just wasted our time and apologized for being a lazy, stupid Nazi.

Two minutes after sending that message, Iman S. Hole told Eileen Dover and I to get our asses in the boardroom. He claimed that I accidentally sent him the electronic sticky instead of Eileen Dover. I knew that was a load of horseshit, because Eileen Dover responded to the message. It was obvious that he was eavesdropping-slash-monitoring our stickies. He told me to go home early without pay. I'm thinking, "Cool, now I can start Happy Hour two hours earlier."

The sad thing was although he was eavesdropping on our messages, he thought I was stupid enough to believe that I accidentally sent the message to him. Eileen Dover confirmed that she did receive the message, so he was indeed eavesdropping on our stickies and playing with his ding-dong while reading the stickies. Five minutes after I left, Eileen Dover told me that his bipolar behavior kicked in. My Bipolar Manager was laughing and prancing around the office like Peter Pan and acting like nothing happened in the boardroom.

"Roses are red, violets are blue. I'm a fucken' nut job, and so am I!"

—Sidney S. Prasad

As much as I couldn't stand working for My Bipolar Manager for forty-plus hours per week, it made it worse that we had to share a train and bus together. My Stupid CEO refused to pay his employees a nickel above slave wages, so everyone had to either drive without insurance or take public transportation with the rest of the lowlifes. So now I had to filter my conversations with my other commuter buddies because Iman S. Hole's supersonic ears were always tuned into my conversations.

"Some see the glass as half empty. I see it as an opportunity to tell the bartender that it's time for a fucken' refill!"

—Sidney S. Prasad

I would always try my best to avoid all company events because everyone that worked there was beneath me. I remember getting out of the Christmas party at a cheesy comedy club one year. I used a bullshit excuse about a religious function that day.

While commuting home on the bus, Iman S. Hole appeared to be listening to some blaring music on his iPod. My buddy, Bill Lowney, asked me what I was doing that weekend. I made the mistake of telling him that I wasn't sure as I have that Saturday night wide open. I told Bill Lowney if I didn't make plans, then I would go to a cougar bar. (I like cougars because most of them are in the union and know how to use their tools, if you know what I mean.) After the bus stopped, the three of us walked onto the platform of the train. Iman S. Hole said, "I am glad that you have Saturday night wide open, because now you can make the Christmas party."

What are the chances that talented creep could tune into my conversation with his headphones blaring music into his ears?

Every workplace has its share of politics. A lot of times, it turns into high school, where small groups of people turn into cliques. Every day working for the man feels like elementary school for me, where I was stuck in a room full of losers that I didn't care for. It's not like high school, where I could choose my classes with my cool friends in them.

Eileen Dover and I had a special bond and our own little clique. We had the privilege of sharing a daily fifteen-minute break together. That's when we would have a jam session of whose getting fat and who is about to get fired. Iman S. Hole would purposely pretend to clean the shelves or organize the fridge while we would be on our break so he could listen to what we were saying.

"Is it normal to be happy during a depression?"

—Sidney S. Prasad

I can't tell you how fucken' frustrating it was to work for a cock with supersonic ears. What kind of ass-monkey gets his yah-yahs from eavesdropping on people bitching about their cheap-ass clients and their fucked-up co-workers? There was even an occasion where Eileen Dover and I were talking about this maniac who switched engines between a sports car and a Honda Civic. Out of nowhere, the warehouse door crashed open and Iman S. Hole accused us of having an inappropriate conversation at the workplace. He gave us a lecture about not talking about sex changes at work. We couldn't get a breath in and tell him that it was a fucken' car engine and not a vagina. I sometimes wonder, if we could communicate telepathically, would Iman S. Hole eavesdrop on our thoughts?

A true sales manager who understands human relations and the psychology of selling would understand that salespeople need to vent to one another. We would spend forty hours per week on the phone, pitching and closing deals. By the time we get home, we don't want to go near a phone. We were so underpaid that we had to take out a second mortgage to buy a fucken' beer after work. We couldn't really tell our significant others about our petty client issues because they thought we were big executives, not salespeople. So the only people we could reach out to were our colleagues during our shitty fifteen-minute break or on a sticky note every now and then.

Personally, if I were managing the sales force, I would encourage all my employees to chat about their problems and create a very positive, supportive, and nurturing environment.

"I told My Bipolar Manager that the North Pole and the South Pole were two extreme polar opposites. It's sort of like *déjà vu*, eh?"

—Sidney S. Prasad

There were times that, while having a telephone conversation with a client, I would tell them about a new website that I discovered or a new gizmo on the market. When I got off the phone and strolled by Iman S. Hole's desk, he would already be on the recommended website or checking the gizmo that I told my client about. I should have played a joke on Iman S. Hole and purposely recommend a fetish party bar or biker hangout to see if he would show up.

What I couldn't stand were those situations where a sales representative was clearly in trouble on the phone, fumbling with their words. The entire office could hear the hesitation of their colleague, but Iman S. Hole conveniently tuned it out. Then, when the sales representative asked him if he heard them talking, he would claim that he never heard them. There were occasions when another departmental manager would bark at me and give me shit. I could have used Iman S. Hole's help to defend me and jump in, as he is supposed to, but all of a sudden he would become temporarily deaf for five minutes.

"You do realize that *The Nutcracker* is a ballet and not a state of mind, right?"

—Sidney S. Prasad

8 WHY ARE THEY SO MISERABLE?

Have you ever dared to ponder why those imbecile bipolar managers are so miserable? In today's challenging economy, we are faced with all types of problems. Even big billionaire tycoons have their issues with fluctuations of commodity prices. Babies have their issues with teething and learning how to walk. Teenagers have their hormonal issues. College students are oversexed and graduate students are undersexed. Married people don't want to have sex. Considering all this, all of us find ways to be happy, regardless of life's challenges.

"No, it's okay, sir, as I don't take things personally. Working for you is the best of both worlds. I get to see you both angry and happy, all in a span of three minutes!"

—Sidney S. Prasad

Do bipolar managers think they are the only people in the world with problems? Part of Iman S. Hole's misery was his victim mentality. He always felt like the world was conspiring against him, including the staff at our office. He did his best to prevent the sales staff from talking to other departments, just in case we tried to organize a petition or walkout, threatening to quit unless he was fired.

But he failed to realize the way we danced around this by coming in super-early and chatting up the other managers to find out the latest dirt on him. We would even make buddies with staff members in other departments and use that line of connection to pass on information. In a sense, it became a self-fulfilling prophecy where we *did* end up conspiring against him.

"Don't ask someone with multiple personalities how many name tags they want. It would be embarrassing if there weren't enough to go around."

—Sidney S. Prasad

There are times when the average person gets really snappy for obvious reasons. If a person is deprived of sleep or food, then it's safe to say they might not be in the best of spirits. But if our bipolar managers instruct us to leave our personal problems at door when arriving to work, then why don't they?

Iman S. Hole might not come out and admit that he was pissed off because he was sexually frustrated due to his girlfriend, boyfriend or blow-up doll not putting out. But he would snap at some innocent employee the first opportunity he got. This one time, Iman S. Hole passed by Eileen Dover's desk and shouted, "Pardon me" to her. Then, he summoned her to the boardroom and gave her shit for muttering under her breath. He wouldn't accept that she preferred to read at a low monotone voice when reading a user-care manual for a buffer. Rather, he was so insecure he thought she was making fun of him.

"My Stupid CEO thought his mom's sisters lived on an ant farm."

—Sidney S. Prasad, My Stupid CEO

I asked my team if they knew anything about Iman S. Hole's personal life. Most of them responded that they didn't know that he *had* a personal life. It was evident Iman S. Hole wasn't from Planet Earth. So I questioned him one day on where he was from and when he arrived to our city. Iman S. Hole apparently moved to town fifteen years ago, just like me. I asked him how often he visited his old buddies and family back home. He told me he has never gone back for a visit since he moved.

That was a red flag in my book for a combination of reasons. I could assume that he must have been, like, the town nerd and didn't want to show his face. I wondered if he might have chopped up his family and had them for dinner during a rampage. I then asked him if he had a roommate, and he said that he lived alone. I read somewhere a long time ago that serial killers live alone and their families aren't traceable.

"Girls, promise me that you won't offer any nuts or crackers to the boss. Because it might just trigger something in his head!"

—Sidney S. Prasad

No one has ever seen Iman S. Hole with a girl. Iman S. Hole claimed that he was active in the dating scene, but I don't know if that includes imaginary dates. He has shown us the odd Facebook picture or online dating website picture of some ugly girl who looked like she belonged to a tribe or something from a *National Geographic* Magazine.

I asked him what type of girls he preferred to date, and he told me the younger, the better. I asked, in respect to being thirty-five years of age, how young does he go, and he said he had no limit. That totally disgusted me, and then my colleagues confirmed that with stories of him hanging out with high-school kids. I can sort of understand why he might be so miserable due to not having any intellectual stimulation in his life. Because I really didn't see some high-school shit having enough worldly experience to intrigue someone old enough to be their father. I pride myself on being an information junkie and only surrounding myself with people of substance.

"My Stupid CEO thought a serial killer ruined his breakfast."

—Sidney S. Prasad, My Stupid CEO

I didn't enjoy commuting to and from work with Iman S. Hole, so that motivated me to take the early-morning train to avoid him. This also motivated me to create a running joke in the office that would be orchestrated every morning that I beat him to work. My sales team and I would have a quick conversation without any eavesdropping or interference by Iman S. Hole. I'd make sure the blinds were open, so I could spot him coming. Then, as soon as I saw him, I would yell, "Everybody wipe the smiles off your faces and go into misery mode." We would have that last chuckle before getting ready for our bipolar manager's mood roller coaster ride. I always wondered, though, if he bugged our office.

Negative energy is disastrous for your health. There are countless times when I could just feel the negative energy that My Bipolar Manager would exude. Walking into the office after coming from a client's place, it felt like someone just died or something. His negativity was so contagious that a lot of us started feeling anxiety and had trouble shaking it off after work. A lot of girls in the office admitted to smoking "funny cigarettes" on a daily basis just to relieve the tension that he forced them to absorb. I am guilty, too, of having to resort to taking down a couple bottles of wine every now and then just to get this loser out of my mind.

"I asked My Bipolar Manager how many mood rings he had broken in the last five minutes."

—Sidney S. Prasad

But the funny thing with Iman S. Hole's volatile bipolar behavior was how radically it would fluctuate. There were several occasions when, after he finished taking a shit on one of us, he would start laughing and acting like Ed McMahon just gave him a check for fifty million dollars. To top it off, he would act like a preacher of positivity. In a strange way, his logic was that if he was in a good mood, then we should forget about the crap he did to us and be in a good mood, too.

Meteorologists can predict the weather and warn us of great hurricanes and storms on the way. There are gifted psychics who can give us hints and warnings about where our life is headed. But no one in the office could really predict when Iman S. Hole's next bipolar temper tantrum was scheduled.

However, there was one exception to that statement. Every Wednesday, there would be a managers' meeting, and ninety-five percent of the time when he came out, he was extra miserable. This was because all the other departmental managers would form an alliance and gang up on him in the boardroom. We would be on our best behavior and avoid our bipolar manager for the remainder of the day.

"Oh shit, the radio is playing 'LET'S GO CRAZY'!"

—Sidney S. Prasad

While consulting at a firm selling oxygenated water in my earlier days of selling, I had the opportunity to work for a veteran old-school salesman who taught me all of his secrets. He told me that whenever I'm in a prospect's office and the meeting is going sour, then look for a vacation picture and just ask a bunch of questions about their last vacation. He said it takes them to a happier place in their mind and makes the client more receptive to purchasing what I'm pitching.

I took that theory to the next step and developed the philosophy that everyone has certain trigger words that affect us in different ways. When I hear or read the name "New York," I get really excited. I start thinking about the women, the nightlife, the entertainment, and that vibe you just can't get anywhere else on the planet that you get in New York. But at the same time, if I hear a certain name that matches a pesky relative of mine, I start feeling some frustration due to a past negative event that took place between us.

"My Stupid CEO got banned from Las Vegas for shitting on the craps table."

—Sidney S. Prasad, My Stupid CEO

My colleagues and I wished that we knew the exact science to Iman S. Hole's nature. We had never seen him work an entire shift without blowing up, as his manic episodes were always spontaneous and unpredictable.

My team member Sheeza Freak once forgot to turn off the lights in the office, partly because she was rushing to the airport for a business trip to Toronto. That was pretty minor, considering the night cleaning crew grabbed the lights on their way out. Three weeks later, someone used the word "Toronto" in a sentence, referring to the Toronto Maple Leafs. This triggered some sort of emotional stimulus in Iman S. Hole, because he opened up a can of whoop-ass on Sheeza Freak. He told her that he forgot to give her shit about not turning off the lights three weeks ago.

"Fuck, my boss is such a downer. He used to manage a mental hospital and got fired for depressing all the patients."

—Sidney S. Prasad

It's quite evident that My Bipolar Manager was harboring some deep-seated emotions, since he was blowing a hissy-fit over something so minor almost a month after the fact, right? Ten minutes later, the bipolar behavior kicked in, and he let Sheeza Freak off early with pay for no apparent reason. Unless it was the guilt kicking in, but only My Bipolar Manager knows the answer.

In my books, there is nothing wrong with being a perfectionist. If we don't crack the whip on ourselves, then no one else will. How else would we achieve our personal goals, right? What we say and do and how we act reflects our personalities from within. If one is purely satisfied with themselves, then they will most likely carry themselves in the most positive manner. If someone is truly miserable and unhappy with themselves, then they will have a shitty outlook on life and act like My Bipolar Manager.

I sometimes wondered if the day would come when a professional army of psychiatrists could gain access to Iman S. Hole's demented dimension and figure out what was really bugging the guy. Maybe if someone could point him toward a good life coach who would mentor him to the right path, then he might be a happier person. But he might also fall into that class of people who just choose to be miserable and destroy all the happiness of everyone around them.

"Never interrupt your bipolar manager when he is about to fire you. Chances are, he might have a sudden mood swing and give you a raise and promotion!"

—Sidney S. Prasad

9 WHO HIRED THESE GUYS?

After working with several bipolar managers in my life and listening to all the stories about all the wacko managers out there, there are several questions that plague me: Who the fuck in their right mind would hire one of these lunatics? Did the Human Resources recruiter bullshit on their resume and have no idea on how to read people? Or was My Stupid CEO, Izzy Cumming, dumber than he looks? Was My Bipolar Manager normal at one point in time? Did anyone else show up for the interview session?

It's scary to imagine how these boneheads get into the company. I sometimes wish we had Homeland Security protecting us against those workplace terrorists. I can totally picture Iman S. Hole chopping up all the interview candidates and hiding their bodies in the dumpster on the day of the interview.

I've worked in boiler rooms where it was common for people to get their buddies hired and hand them a supervisor position. Usually, the people hired paid tribute back by buying their buddies drinks and other party-favors on paydays. But Iman S. Hole isn't capable of keeping an imaginary friend and the entire company couldn't stand him, so that wouldn't be the case. Maybe he greased someone with money to get his foot in the door. No, that couldn't be it, because if you'd seen the way this guy fucken' dressed, you would agree that Walmart was too upscale for him.

"You have no control of what people think of you, but you have full control of what you think of yourself!"

—Sidney S. Prasad

Some bipolar managers are somewhat lucky in their own special way, as a lot of them are owner-operators of their businesses. I can only speculate that they were normal at some point in time and it was the fluctuations of business and competition that fucked them up. There are jerks out there who take two parking spaces to park their Hot rods. Their justification is that if you owned one of those babies, you would do the same thing. Maybe that is the philosophy of owner-operator bipolar managers.

If an entire staff room full of people can unanimously agree that their manager is bipolar, then I can't fathom how the recruiter couldn't figure it out. Most recruiters get hundreds of resumes emailed, faxed, and dropped off to them. They spend countless hours interviewing desperate people, willing to work for pennies. With that in mind, you figure that their intuition would guide them in the right direction when making a decision about a suitable candidate. It just blows my mind during the aftermath whenever a bipolar manager was dismissed. Senior management would comment that the bipolar manager must have slipped through the cracks.

"Is it O.K. if I sit here, or is this your imaginary friend's spot?"

—Sidney S. Prasad

There are those odd tales of people who were sane and normal once upon a time. However, they stayed in their company way too long, and now they are a couple French fries short of a combo. What I'm trying to get to is that there are people who start out cool and hip, but after a couple years of doing the same grind, they eventually get promoted to manager. However, they are not the same person as they were when they first got into the company. Plus, all their bipolar managers rubbed off on them. I couldn't see Iman S. Hole ever being cool. I can see him having temper tantrums in preschool and pissing off all the little shits because someone stole his chair at the arts and crafts table.

"The motel requires me to check out at 11:00 AM. I wonder what is check-out time at the mental hospital for My Bipolar Manager?"

—Sidney S. Prasad

If we dismiss the fact that Iman S. Hole didn't kill anyone to get hired, and we cancel the theory of him bribing someone to get in here, then there are only a couple of viable scenarios left. I'm not sure if My Stupid CEO goes both ways or not, but it wouldn't surprise me. He's got some man-boobies and really likes little boys, but his wife throws me off. We have all heard stories of people giving sexual favors to the boss in order to secure a job or promotion. I did see some kneepads in Iman S. Hole's briefcase, but no rollerblades.

Hmm, but hold on… believe it or not, My Stupid CEO's wife, named Anita Dyck, earned the position as Vice President by pretending she was a White House intern, if you know what I mean. Eventually, she got herself pregnant and stonewalled My Stupid CEO into marrying her and surrendering half the company to her. If you talk to this bitch, she gives new meaning to the word "stupid." Anita Dyck was so stupid that, one day, she got locked in the toilet and pissed herself. So I can't see My Stupid CEO, Izzy Cumming, making the same mistake twice, unless he is dumber than his ugly wife.

"I caught my psycho boss in the lost-and-found box, looking for his mind."

—Sidney S. Prasad

It really wouldn't surprise me if Iman S. Hole and my other bipolar managers of the past fabricated and embellished their resumes. I can totally see these losers using their favorite bartenders-slash-psychologists from the pub to be their references. Fuck, the bartenders are not going to think twice about it as long as they keep tipping them and continue showing up twice a day to drown their sorrows. Or maybe the bipolar managers used their drinking buddies to vouch for them being sane. Perhaps all of the bipolar manager's co-workers from their last jobs were so fucken' desperate to get rid of these fucks that they all gave a kick-ass reference so someone else would inherit their problem.

"My Stupid CEO was curious what time 7-11 closed."

—Sidney S. Prasad, My Stupid CEO

From observing many bipolar managers, it is quite evident that they are the masters of the art of bullshitting. This is especially true when they are lying for something to pan out in their favor. Due to their bipolar nature, they can switch moods like a six-speed transmission on a Corvette. For example, whenever Iman S. Hole was speaking to My Stupid CEO or one of the suit dummies from the executive team, he would actually come across normal. Even if he had just finished shitting on someone for twenty minutes when the CEO called him, you wouldn't be able to detect even one iota of anger or hostility in his voice.

So I imagine that Iman S. Hole did his best acting job during his interview and spread that bullshit really thick and deep. This sort of reinforces the notion that serial killers are known to look someone in the eye when they lie and not flinch once.

"My Stupid CEO put condoms on his ears to avoid hearing aids."

—Sidney S. Prasad, My Stupid CEO

Depending on the company structure, it's common for an organization to have a manager or two interview a candidate and then have the CEO step in for the final deal-making interview. That was the case for Iman S. Hole. I sometimes pondered if he blackmailed My Stupid CEO or put a gun to his head to get the job.

He later admitted to me the stunt that he pulled to become My Bipolar Manager. His previous employer caught on that he was a train wreck and turfed him out on the street. However, the CEO who fired him, named Eaton Bush, was well known, highly respected, and written up in every business magazine. My Stupid CEO belonged to an Entrepreneurs Club, and Eaton Bush was a member of the same group. My Stupid CEO was a hero in his own mind and thought he was admired and well-liked around town as well. However, in reality, he was the laughingstock of the business community. Anyway, My Bipolar Manager told My Stupid CEO that he was the right-hand man of Eaton Bush, and that he wanted to come aboard because he saw a bigger growth opportunity in this firm. So, throwing around Eaton Bush's name got him into our firm with no reference check.

"Take a vacation from your problems and give yourself permission to enjoy the present moment!"

—Sidney S. Prasad

87

After he shared that story with me, I had to test the waters and dig a little deeper. I questioned Iman S. Hole about his previous job as a general manager for a pest control company. I asked him, "Why would you leave the position after five years?" He told me without any remorse that he was promised a vice president position as soon the acting vice president retired. Then, after waiting years for the guy to drop dead or retire, he went into the office and pulled a Rambo. Basically, he jumped on the guy's desk, grabbed him by his shirt, and confronted him about why he wouldn't fucken' retire. Instantly, he was fired, and you have to be bipolar to pull that off.

"What's more valuable in your book, a minute of anger or a minute of happiness?"

—Sidney S. Prasad

10 GET OUT AND GET EVEN!

After being enlightened by the tales of My Bipolar Manager, I'm quite confident that you would agree that Iman S. Hole and the other fuck-head managers displayed some bipolar-ass behavior in their own unique style. Some people might find it entertaining to work for that sort of personality type, while others find it emotionally draining. Making a living and trying to stay afloat is a major challenge these days, especially with the current state of our economy. Life at the workplace becomes even more challenging when one is stuck in a hostile environment.

Personal happiness is sometimes considered a rare commodity. Some people just tie their hands together and put themselves at the mercy of their organization. They sacrifice their own livelihoods and peace of mind and tolerate the bullshit of their bipolar managers for the duration of their contract. This is not healthy for your organization, as there is a high probability that you, too, will turn into a bipolar manager one day, based on the misery you went through. However, career aside, this is even more damaging to your personal health.

"I pissed off My Bipolar Manager by asking him what he takes with his medicine."

—Sidney S. Prasad

Based on mathematical calculations, the average person spends a little more than one-third of their life at work. A lot of people are accustomed to making personal sacrifices and cutting down their luxuries to suit a lower pay-scale. Some people report that their jobs are stressful because their customers beat them up on a daily basis. Most employees can accept their dog shit wages and handle the customer bullshit. But they say it would be like night and day if their bipolar managers were fired or reprogrammed to act normal.

"The good news is that I have more than enough money to last me the rest of my life. The bad news is the doctor told me that I only have one day left to live."

—Sidney S. Prasad

Selling janitorial supplies for a tiny, measly wage took a toll on my colleagues' personal lifestyles as well as my own. We all agreed that we were earning at least forty percent less than at our previous jobs. It made it worse that we knew that exact amount of profit that we were making for My Stupid CEO.

We would all average out about seventy-five phone calls per day, and most of those calls weren't as friendly as we would hope them to be. But, being professional salespeople, we knew it was part of the territory and developed thick skin long ago. Having a close work relationship within the sales team, we would always have the inside scoop on how each of us was feeling. Collectively, we would take random sick days to go on job interviews with prospective employers. We would also take random sick days just to have a vacation from our bipolar manager. We all agreed on one thing universally: we wouldn't mind our low-paying, stressful job if our bipolar manager weren't part of our organization. He was pretty much the main factor driving all of us bonkers.

"I have always wondered if people who can communicate telepathically ever engage in mind sex."

—Sidney S. Prasad, Plenty Of Freaks: Are You Sold On Online Dating?

I remember that by 3:00 PM every Sunday, I would be extremely pissed off, because I knew the party was over. As much as I tried not to think about it, every time I would look at the clock, it would feel like a New Year's Eve countdown. I would be thinking, "Okay, in less than fifteen-and-a-half hours, I am going to be face to face with that moron." I can't tell you how many countless times I accidentally cut or burnt myself preparing breakfast because of the anxiety of going to work and seeing My Bipolar Manager. There were even times where I would hold on to the doorknob of my front door for, like, half an hour because I didn't want to go to work and see that asshole.

"The restaurant sign said 'Dinner Anytime,' so my psychotic boss asked for the Last Supper."

—Sidney S. Prasad

After being emotionally drained for over two-and-a-half years by My Bipolar Manager, I wouldn't wish that dramatic experience on my worst enemy. Working in a dysfunctional environment is similar to being in a communist prison. There would be days where I would wanted to reach into my lunch bag and grab a spoon, then start digging a tunnel to the next prospective employer's workplace.

One thing that anyone can do in this situation is to get out and get even and to take advantage of the company Rolodex. For example, if you are a salesperson and you get an expense account, make a habit of spending your Stupid CEO's money on a "life preserver" for yourself. I'm talking about giving gifts and incentives to clients who you could see being your next prospective employer. There's a certain level of professionalism we have to maintain with our clients. But we also have those clients who are like our best friends that we can share our frustrations with. There are a lot of happy-ending stories where one of those clients took someone out of their misery and hired them.

"I love it how women maintain eye contact throughout dinner and look away when the check comes."

—Sidney S. Prasad, Plenty Of Freaks: Are You Sold On Online dating?

If you are stuck in a situation where your bipolar manager owns the company, there are a few dirty tricks you can do to get even. Observe everything the company is doing and look for violations, like making sure everyone is wearing steel-toed boots and following state warehouse regulations. Try to catch someone not wearing proper safety gear, such as a hairnet, reflective vest, or protective gloves. Record the dates and times, and then report it to the proper authorities. Also, peek into the first-aid kit and make sure it's up-to-date, as that is a violation too. Make sure the fire extinguishers are in working condition; the owner can receive a fine for that, as well.

If there are cash incentives being dispersed to employees, then share that information with the Internal Revenue Service. Look for mousetraps and any sort of health violation to catch your employer with. Nitpick with anything you can possibly get them in shit with. Try to stay up-to-date with labor board regulations and current Human Rights laws.

"A jail is a prison for some while a mind is a prison for others."

—Sidney S. Prasad

Then, when you are ready to make your exit, create a script that will humiliate your bipolar manager and put him in his place. If he owns the joint, he will be stuck facing all of his employees with humiliation every day until he sells the place or goes bankrupt.

The final icing on the cake is take advantage of the Internet to give some negative publicity to the company. Check out websites such as ratemyemployer.com and verbalize all the shit that asshole put you through. It's a very therapeutic thought, knowing that you can prevent a couple of other people following your footsteps right? My Stupid CEO, Izzy Cumming, has a Google Alert set up so he gets an email notification anytime there is anything in cyberspace good or bad said about him or about his shitty ass company. Keeping this in mind, it would really piss off your bipolar manager if you started expressing your feelings on a blog or some tweets on a social media website.

"If I ask you to go Dutch, are you going to dump me?"

—Sidney S. Prasad, Plenty Of Freaks: Are You Sold On Online Dating?

If your bipolar manager is sort of a middle manager who is governed by a Stupid CEO and some suit dummies, then your strategy may be a little different. The first rule to incorporate is survival of the fittest. Secure your own meal ticket. Try to get someone else to fight your battles for you without letting them know that they are your bitch. Every time one of your colleagues comes out of the boardroom in tears, empathetically sympathize with them and then ask them what they are going to do about it. Fill their mind with stories of how other people took a stand and acted bold. Maybe one of the suit dummies or your Stupid CEO may just listen to their crying plea and fire your bipolar manager. Fighting is awesome when you don't get your own hands dirty.

"Look I know you're from a nut farm, but can you try to keep your mind like a stable?"

—Sidney S. Prasad

Two of my colleagues, Wilma Dickfit and Nida Lyte, were smart. They jumped ship within three months of working for My Bipolar Manager. Then, there was a Brazilian beauty named Sue Shee who took his shit for six months before caving. But the smartest cookie that I'd seen was Pat Hiscock. This chick was more outspoken than a New York attorney and she had balls bigger than grapefruits, in a metaphoric sense. She fought back tooth-and-nail each time she was hauled into the boardroom; mind you, this was during her first week. During her second week, she started circulating a petition to various people in our company in a campaign to take Iman S. Hole down. Unfortunately, we had a rat among our team who tipped off My Bipolar Manager and got her fired. The next day, a new policy was implemented that no one from our team was allowed to leave our section, which was in line of sight and earshot of Iman S. Hole. Any correspondence with another department had to be done by telephone or email, because he had access to tapping both of those communication devices. So we were pretty much fucked for the next year in terms of starting another revolution.

"Oh, you got tickets for the ball game. So I guess you are sitting in the asshole section, with the rest of your clan?"

—Sidney S. Prasad

A year later, My Stupid CEO hired this guy who looked like O.J. Simpson that My Stupid CEO had a man-crush on. His name was Harry Cox, and he was so full of shit that his eyes were brown. But for some reason, all the idiots in my office, including My Stupid CEO, didn't spot it. Harry Cox would spend an entire shift walking around with his coffee in one hand and his other hand in his pocket and get away with it. The sad thing was My Stupid CEO, Izzy Cumming, thought he was the best thing since sliced bread. He created an anonymous survey for employee feedback about their work environment. Some people spoke up, but I chose my words carefully because Iman S. Hole tipped me off, telling me that he was in charge of electronically retrieving the surveys and printing them to Harry Cox.

"People spend one third of their life at work. Fuck, that's a scary thought!"

—Sidney S. Prasad

I decided to say "fuck this bullshit" and give myself a little break. I called Iman S. Hole one night and announced that a close family member had died. I said that, due to religious rituals, I required a two-week leave from work. He bought my bullshit and granted me two weeks to get drunk, get laid, and conspire against him. What a stupid fuck, I thought, because he even sent me a bereavement bouquet of flowers.

When I got back, all well rested, there was another survey. This time, it was an old-fashioned type where we had to use a pen and write long essay answers. We were required to evaluate our boss, and then hand it to him. My co-workers warned me that if I put anything negative, I would be hauled into the boardroom. I decided to take another route and play a dirty card. I gave My Bipolar Manager an excellent review and typed out ten pages of statements referring to what a wonderful guy he was. I even stressed that he was well suited as a candidate to become our company's next vice president. My strategy with pulling this off was to get the suspicion off me. I wanted Iman S. Hole to think that he could actually trust me and I wouldn't fuck him over when he was not looking.

"Did you know it takes more facial muscles to make a frown then it does to make a smile?"

—Sidney S. Prasad

Sure enough, this reverse-psychology bullshit worked and I earned his trust. For the next little while, Iman S. Hole would share classified information with me that I would use it to my advantage. During my downtime, I would secretly campaign against My Bipolar Manager and see who was for him and who was against him. It didn't take long to find out the entire company despised him. I would do my best to motivate and encourage all my colleagues to get even or get out.

Finally, Jean Poole secured a job at the office of one of her clients and gave her notice. Iman S. Hole was paranoid that she would brainwash the rest of us into hating him during her final two weeks. So he convinced My Stupid CEO to pay out her severance and fire Jean Poole on the spot.

"I'm not unemployed, but I am an entrepreneur!"

—Sidney S. Prasad

Jean Poole gladly took the payout and left without a fight. Then, we all raided her desk and stocked up on office supplies and tampons. Cleverly, My Stupid CEO's best and only friend, Wayne Kerr, was one of the suit dummies on the executive team. Jean Poole managed to convince Wayne Kerr to go for drinks with her and spilled her guts out on what Iman S. Hole has done to her colleagues' morale. Magically, in the weeks that followed, every single person in the company was given a one-on-one meeting with Harry Cox to vocalize their concerns about Iman S. Hole.

Harry Cox enjoyed this because now he had all the fucken' time to drink his coffee and bullshit with the staff. I told my colleagues in advance to write themselves detailed letters with dates and times and highlight that shit. This was to shed light on all the bipolar activity that we had encountered, from the time we entered the company right up to the meeting. I could have taken a whole fucken' file cabinet with me with all the shit I had on Iman S. Hole, but I ended up taking an accordion file box.

My thirty-minute session turned into a two-hour-and-forty-five-minute meeting. I could have sat there until midnight talking about past events. However, I could tell that Harry Cox was hungry and wanted to go do a couple rounds at the neighborhood buffet.

"Did you ever wonder why unemployed people and welfare recipients never get to be contestants on game shows? Because they could really use the fucken' money!"

—Sidney S. Prasad

The ball finally started rolling and the universe unraveled a path of justice for us. You can definitely apply this to your workplace and see if your upper management would be receptive to using the survey concept. But I suggest that the drop box for the survey should have limited classified access, especially to your bipolar manager. If your colleagues and yourself suggest even a five-minute meeting with Your Stupid CEO or an executive suit dummy, then the universe may conspire to work with you as well.

I never knew that I would witness a day of reckoning. After two-and-a-half years, My Bipolar Manager finally got fired for creating a hostile environment. About fucken' time, don't you think?

A large celebration broke out, and it was like heaven on earth at the workplace. This sort of reminded me of the celebrations shown on the news when Saddam Hussein was taken out of power. The weeks that followed were quite peaceful, and our happiness level was at an all-time high. It was an amazing feeling to come to work and not get dragged down by My Bipolar Manager's negativity and depression.

My Stupid CEO's wife, Anita Dyck, decided that she was sick of banging the mailman and wanted to come back to work. Like I mentioned earlier, she was fucken' dumber than a doorknob and completely useless. Every time I would ask her a question, she would ask me what I thought. "If I knew the fucken' answer, then I wouldn't be asking your dumb ass," I thought.

"My sales manager couldn't sell shit to a toilet paper factory if his life depended on it!"

—Sidney S. Prasad

A year in advance, I promised myself that I would leave the company. But I told myself that I would only leave after I witnessed the fall of My Bipolar Manager. I always knew in my heart it would make an interesting story to share. I really didn't give a shit about leaving on a bad note and burning bridges. I waited for the right moment to make my exit and write the great American novel.

The day finally came when Anita Dyck asked me to change my desk with an ex-crackhead named Sharon Needles. Sharon Needles claimed that she had a seasonal disorder and needed my window spot. This was convenient, I thought, considering it was a record-high summer, and who wouldn't want a window seat to absorb some sunshine. I told Anita Dyck that she could gladly have my chair after she pulls it out of her ass. My final words to Anita Dyck were, "Take your job, and kiss my sweet brown ass!"

But, wait! The story doesn't have to end here. If you have enjoyed reading about My Bipolar Manager, then you are going to love my book about the idiot who hired him, *My Stupid CEO*.

"I always tip my bartender; do you tip your pharmacist?"

—Sidney S. Prasad

ABOUT THE AUTHOR

Sidney S. Prasad is an author who is on a quest to make the world laugh. His work is focused on entertaining people with his dry-humored novels. Sidney S. Prasad personally believes laughter is the best cure for all of life's ups and downs.

Some other humorous books written by Sidney S. Prasad include:

How To Piss Off A Telemarketer,

My Stupid CEO,

Don't Ask Dumb Questions!,

Plenty Of Freaks: Are You Sold On Online Dating?

Corny Names & Stupid Places,

Misfortune Cookies,

and

Telemarketer's Revenge: The Customer Is Always Wrong, Bitch!